Praise be to the Lord
thy God.
Blessed be God
Forever.
Thank the Lord for any
good in your life.......
Then claim the help you
need from the Lord and
see the goodness of
God.

Thank You My Lord,
My God.
Blessed Be God Forever

Psalm 46:10 "Be still, and know that I
am God…"

By Susan Prinz

Let the goodness of God sink down into the depth of your very soul knowing that;
"I am the Lord, and there is none else, there is no God beside me:"

Isaiah 45:5

Praise and thank you God,
I am loving the feeling and
accept being healthy, happy and
confident now this moment
without delay. I am. It is done,
Thank you Father.

Praise and thank you God,
I am loving the feeling and
accept being strong, powerful
and confident now this moment
without delay. I am. It is done,
Thank you Father.

Praise and thank you God,
I am loving the feeling and
accept being fearless, free and
confident now this moment
without delay. I am. It is done,
Thank you Father.

Praise and thank you God,
I am loving the feeling and
accept being at peace, calm and
confident now this moment
without delay. I am. It is done,
Thank you Father.

Praise and thank you God,
I am loving the feeling and
accept being whole and perfect
with confidence now this moment
without delay. I am. It is done,
Thank you Father.

Praise and thank you God,
I am loving the feeling and
accept being blessed and
confident now this moment
without delay. I am. It is done,
Thank you Father.

Praise and thank you God,
I am loving the feeling and
accept being cleansed and pure
now this moment without delay. I
am. It is done, Thank you
Father.

～～✕～～

Praise and thank you God,
I am loving the feeling and
accept being happy, joyous and
confident now this moment
without delay. I am. It is done,
Thank you Father.

Praise and thank you God,
I am loving the feeling and
accept being protected, safe,
secure and confident now this
moment without delay. I am. It is
done, Thank you Father.

⌘

Praise and thank you God,
I am loving the feeling and
accept being successful and
confident now this moment
without delay. I am. It is done,
Thank you Father.

Praise and thank you God,
I am loving the feeling and
accept being wealthy and
confident now this moment
without delay. I am. It is done,
Thank you Father.

Praise and thank you God,
I am loving the feeling and
accept being full of faith, trust
and confidence now this moment
without delay. I am. It is done,
Thank you Father.

Praise and thank you God,
I am loving the feeling and accept being forgiven by God now this moment without delay. I am. It is done, Thank you Father.

Praise and thank you God,
I am loving the feeling and accept being patient with myself and others now this moment without delay. I am. It is done, Thank you Father.

Praise and thank you God,
I am loving the feeling and
accept being balanced in all
areas of my life now this
moment without delay. I am. It is
done, Thank you Father.

———⁓✕⁓———

Praise and thank you God,
I am loving the feeling and
accept being healed and blessed
by God now this moment without
delay. I am. It is done, Thank
you Father.

Praise and thank you God,
I am loving the feeling and accept being free now without delay. I am. It is done, Thank you Father.

Praise and thank you God,
I am loving the feeling and accept being forgiven by God now this moment without delay. I am. It is done, Thank you Father.

Praise and thank you God,
I am loving the feeling and
accept perfect self-control of my
thoughts and feelings now this
moment without delay. I am. It is
done, Thank you Father.

⁂

Praise and thank you God,
I am loving the feeling and
accept being beautiful and
confident now this moment
without delay. I am. It is done,
Thank you Father.

Praise and thank you God,
I am loving the feeling and
accept being restored with the
joy of my salvation now this
moment without delay. I am. It is
done, Thank you Father.

Praise and thank you God,
I am loving the feeling and
accept being full of life, energy,
vitality, and confident now this
moment without delay. I am. It is
done, Thank you Father.

Praise and thank you God,
I am loving the feeling and
accept being full of happiness,
joy and confident now this
moment without delay. I am. It is
done, Thank you Father.

Praise and thank you God,
I am loving the feeling and
accept always thinking rightly,
GODS perfect loving thoughts,
words and deeds now this
moment without delay. I am. It is
done, Thank you Father.

Praise and thank you God,
I am loving the feeling and
accept being full of peace,
harmony and confidence now this
moment without delay. I am. It is
done, Thank you Father.

Praise and thank you God,
I am loving the feeling and
accept being free of the
condemnation and judgement of
myself and others now this
moment without delay. I am. It is
done, Thank you Father.

Praise and thank you God,
I am loving the feeling and
accept being free, limitless,
boundless now this moment
without delay. I am. It is done,
Thank you Father.

Praise and thank you God,
I am loving the feeling and
accept having freedom of cares
now this moment without delay. I
am. It is done, Thank you
Father.

Praise and thank you God,
I am loving the feeling and
accept being divinely lead,
guided and inspired from on high
now this moment without delay. I
am. It is done, Thank you
Father.

⁓⤬⁓

Praise and thank you God,
I am loving the feeling and
accept being supplied by God
now this moment without delay. I
am. It is done, Thank you
Father.

Praise and thank you God,
I am loving the feeling and accept being supplied by God and made pure, radiant and confident now this moment without delay. I am. It is done, Thank you Father.

⸺⸺❧⸺⸺

Praise and thank you God,
I am loving the feeling and accept being supplied by God and made whole every whit now this moment without delay. I am. It is done, Thank you Father.

Praise and thank you God,
I am loving the feeling and accept being supplied by God and the whole armor of God protects me now this moment without delay. I am. It is done, Thank you Father.

Praise and thank you God,
I am loving the feeling and accept Gods mercy and goodness will follow me always now this moment without delay. I am. It is done, Thank you Father.

Praise and thank you God,
I am loving the feeling and
accept being supplied by God
with faith and courage now this
moment without delay. I am. It is
done, Thank you Father.

Praise and thank you God,
I am loving the feeling and
accept being supplied by God
with love towards all people now
this moment without delay. I am.
It is done, Thank you Father.

Praise and thank you God,
I am loving the feeling and accept only hearing the good about myself and others that fill my heart with love now this moment without delay. I am. It is done, Thank you Father.

Praise and thank you God,
I am loving the feeling and accept only expecting the best now this moment without delay. I am. It is done, Thank you Father.

Praise and thank you God,
I am loving the feeling and accept being consciously awakened in Gods truth now this moment without delay. I am. It is done, Thank you Father.

Praise and thank you God,
I am loving the feeling and accept hearing the good news now this moment without delay. I am. It is done, Thank you Father.

Praise and thank you God,
I am loving the feeling and accept awakening my creativity to bring happiness and joy into my life and to those around me now this moment without delay. I am. It is done, Thank you Father.

***

Praise and thank you God,
I am loving the feeling and accept only having a clear and ordered mind now this moment without delay. I am. It is done, Thank you Father.

Praise and thank you God,
I am loving the feeling and
accept total indifference to
suggestions that are not pleasing
to me now this moment without
delay. I am. It is done, Thank
you Father.

Praise and thank you God,
I am loving the feeling and
accept my desires as gifts from
God that have the power and
plan for success now this
moment without delay. I am. It is
done, Thank you Father.

Praise and thank you God,
I am loving the feeling and
accept always praising and
thanking God for the goodness of
the Lord now this moment
without delay. I am. It is done,
Thank you Father.

Praise and thank you God,
I am loving the feeling and
accept only placing my attention
on the solution in all areas of my
life now this moment without
delay. I am. It is done, Thank
you Father.

Praise and thank you God,
I am loving the feeling and
accept being at rest and calm
knowing all things are possible
with God now this moment
without delay. I am. It is done,
Thank you Father.

~~~⌘~~~

Praise and thank you God,
I am loving the feeling and
accept being surrounded by
peace, harmony and happiness in
all areas of my life now this
moment without delay. I am. It
is done, Thank you Father.

Praise and thank you God,
I am loving the feeling and accept being surrounded by joy, love and laughter in all areas of my life now this moment without delay. I am. It is done, Thank you Father.

Praise and thank you God,
I am loving the feeling and accept being surrounded by Gods blessings in all areas of my life now this moment without delay. I am. It is done, Thank you Father.

Praise and thank you God,
I am loving the feeling and
accept being thankful God is
providing for my family and loved
ones in all areas now this
moment without delay. I am. It is
done, Thank you Father.

Praise and thank you God,
I am loving the feeling and
accept God is protecting my
family and loved ones now this
moment without delay. I am. It is
done, Thank you Father.

Praise and thank you God,
I am loving the feeling and
accept being thankful only good
can come to me in all areas of
my life now this moment without
delay. I am. It is done, Thank
you Father.

Praise and thank you God,
I am loving the feeling and
accept being passionate, fulfilled
and complete in all areas of my
life now this moment without
delay. I am. It is done, Thank
you Father.

Praise and thank you God,
I am loving the feeling and
accept being surrounded by Gods
goodness and mercy in all areas
of my life now this moment
without delay. I am. It is done,
Thank you Father.

—⁓∞⁓—

Praise and thank you God,
I am loving the feeling and
accept placing all things into the
hands of God in all areas of my
life now this moment without
delay. I am. It is done, Thank
you Father.

Praise and thank you God,
I am loving the feeling and
accept being kind, thoughtful and
generous in all areas of my life
now this moment without delay. I
am. It is done, Thank you
Father.

Praise and thank you God,
I am loving the feeling and
accept being sweet, gentle and
childlike in spirit in all areas of
my life now this moment without
delay. I am. It is done, Thank
you Father.

Praise and thank you God,
I am loving the feeling and
accept being surrounded by
happy, joyous, loving people and
things in all areas of my life now
this moment without delay. I am.
It is done, Thank you Father.

Praise and thank you God,
I am loving the feeling and
accept being at peace and calm
in all areas of my life now this
moment without delay. I am. It is
done, Thank you Father.

Praise and thank you God,
I am loving the feeling and accept
being joyous claiming all good
things in all areas of my life now
this moment without delay. I am.
It is done, Thank you Father.

Praise and thank you God,
I am feeling and accept Gods
healing presence and infinite
power flowing through me now
and has made me whole every
whit this very moment without
delay. I am. It is done, Thank you
Father.

Praise and thank you God,
I am loving the feeling and
accept only words, ideas,
thoughts, feelings, beliefs into
my conscious and subconscious
mind that heals, blesses,
inspires, and fills my heart with
love now this moment without
delay. I am. It is done, Thank
you Father.

I hope this book helps you to focus your attention and awareness on whatever changes you would like to make to improve your life. I would suggest that you pick out areas that apply to your life and choose one thing daily that you repetitively say over and over in your mind until it becomes a natural feeling in your awareness and until you see it manifesting in your life. May God bless you and your loved ones now and forever.

I would like to thank my wonderful, loving husband Mark Campbell for all his help in the production of this book.

www.ingramcontent.com/pod-product-compliance
Lightning Source LLC
Chambersburg PA
CBHW061654050426
42443CB00027B/3290